HOUSES

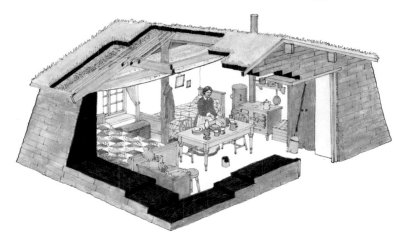

HABITATS & HOME LIFE

Series Editor:
David Salariya was born in Dundee, Scotland, where he studied illustration and printmaking, concentrating on book design in his postgraduate year. He has illustrated a wide range of books on botanical, historical and mythical subjects. He has designed and created many new series of children's books for publishers worldwide. In 1989, he established his own publishing company, The Salariya Book Company Ltd. He lives in Brighton with his wife, the illustrator Shirley Willis.

Author:
Fiona Macdonald studied history at Cambridge University and at the University of East Anglia, where she is a part-time tutor. She has written many books for children on historical topics, including *Cities* in the *Timelines* series, and *How Would You Survive as an Aztec?*

Consultant:
Dr. Tom Williamson studied history and archaeology at Cambridge University and is now Lecturer in Landscape History at the University of East Anglia. He has written many books and has appeared on radio and television.

First published in the United States in 1994 by Franklin Watts

Series Editor	David Salariya
Senior Editor	Ruth Nason
Book Editor	Jenny Millington
Consultant	Dr. Tom Williamson
Artists	David Antram
	Mark Bergin
	Catherine Constable
	John James
	Deborah Kindred
	Mark Peppé
	Gerald Wood

Artists
David Antram p 34-35, p 36-37, p 38-39; **Mark Bergin** p 14-15, p 20-21, p 22-23; **Catherine Constable** p 6-7, p 24-25; **John James** p 8-9, p 10-11; **Deborah Kindred** p 26-27, p 28-29, p 42-43; **Mark Peppé** p 18-19, p 32-33; **Gerald Wood** p 12-13, p 16-17, p 30-31.

Franklin Watts
95 Madison Avenue
New York, NY 10016

© The Salariya Book Company Ltd MCMXCIV

Library of Congress Cataloging-in-Publication Data
Macdonald, Fiona.
    Houses : habitats & home life / written by Fiona Macdonald : created & designed by David Salariya.
        p.   cm. -- (Timelines)
    Includes index.
    ISBN 0-531-14332-5 (lib. bdg.). -- ISBN 0-531-15719-9 (pbk.)
    1. Dwellings--History--Juvenile literature. 2. Vernacular architecture--History--Juvenile literature. 3. Manners and customs -History--Juvenile literature. [1. Dwellings--History.]
I. Salariya, David. II. Title. III. Series: Timelines (Franklin Watts, inc.)
GT172.M33 1994   94-14040
392'.3--dc20   CIP
                                            AC

Printed in Belgium

TIMELINES
HOUSES

HABITATS & HOME LIFE

Written by
FIONA MACDONALD

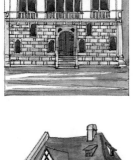

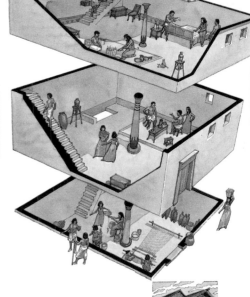

Created & Designed by
DAVID SALARIYA

FRANKLIN WATTS

New York • Chicago • London • Toronto • Sydney

CONTENTS

THE FIRST HOUSES

MANY YEARS AGO, people believed that the earliest humans were "cavemen" – that is, beings who were too ignorant and primitive to build houses, but who lived in caves instead. Today we know that this image of early humans is wrong. They were skillful hunters who knew how to make tools out of stones and bones – archaeologists have found the remains.

△ OVAL HUT at Terra Amata, in southern France, made of twigs and brushwood, of around 300,000 B.C.

▷ HUTS made of skins sewn together and weighted down with animal bones were made by Paleolithic hunters between 35,000 and 10,000 B.C. The harsh Ice Age climate meant that there were no trees to provide wood for building. Remains of huts like these have been found on open steppes in Russia, Ukraine, and the Czech Republic.

△ AROUND 12,000 years ago, hunters built "longhouses" (tents) for winter shelter. Each tent, made of skin and timber, housed several families.

The idea that the earliest humans lived only in caves can also be shown to be wrong. It is partly common sense – in many parts of the world where early human skeletons have been found, there are no caves. But there is also evidence that early people built houses. Archaeologists have excavated traces of many different types of buildings dating from over 300,000 years ago. They believe that remains of many more early homes may be discovered one day.

▽ SHELTERS for fishing families at Lepenski Vir, Yugoslavia, were made of wood covered with turf, 5000–4600 B.C.

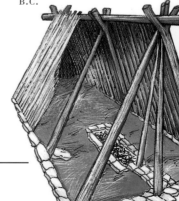

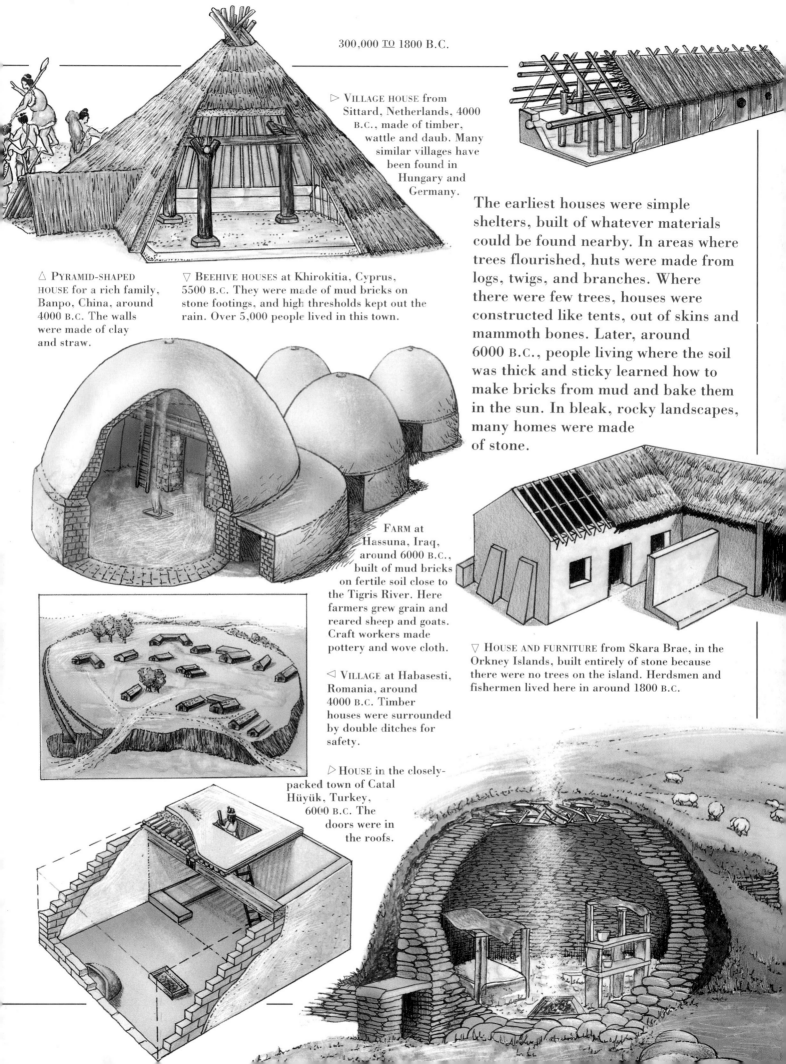

▷ VILLAGE HOUSE from Sittard, Netherlands, 4000 B.C., made of timber, wattle and daub. Many similar villages have been found in Hungary and Germany.

△ PYRAMID-SHAPED HOUSE for a rich family, Banpo, China, around 4000 B.C. The walls were made of clay and straw.

▽ BEEHIVE HOUSES at Khirokitia, Cyprus, 5500 B.C. They were made of mud bricks on stone footings, and high thresholds kept out the rain. Over 5,000 people lived in this town.

The earliest houses were simple shelters, built of whatever materials could be found nearby. In areas where trees flourished, huts were made from logs, twigs, and branches. Where there were few trees, houses were constructed like tents, out of skins and mammoth bones. Later, around 6000 B.C., people living where the soil was thick and sticky learned how to make bricks from mud and bake them in the sun. In bleak, rocky landscapes, many homes were made of stone.

▷ FARM at Hassuna, Iraq, around 6000 B.C., built of mud bricks on fertile soil close to the Tigris River. Here farmers grew grain and reared sheep and goats. Craft workers made pottery and wove cloth.

◁ VILLAGE at Habasesti, Romania, around 4000 B.C. Timber houses were surrounded by double ditches for safety.

▷ HOUSE in the closely-packed town of Catal Hüyük, Turkey, 6000 B.C. The doors were in the roofs.

▽ HOUSE AND FURNITURE from Skara Brae, in the Orkney Islands, built entirely of stone because there were no trees on the island. Herdsmen and fishermen lived here in around 1800 B.C.

EGYPT AND GREECE

Palm-thatched roof

Oven

Kitchen

Living room

A HOUSE IS MORE than just somewhere to shelter from the weather. It can be a fortress or a factory, a shop or a center of government. It can be a place where you entertain friends and colleagues, or a way of displaying your taste, your status, and your wealth.

Roof space used for work and play

Entrance hall

Bedroom and storeroom

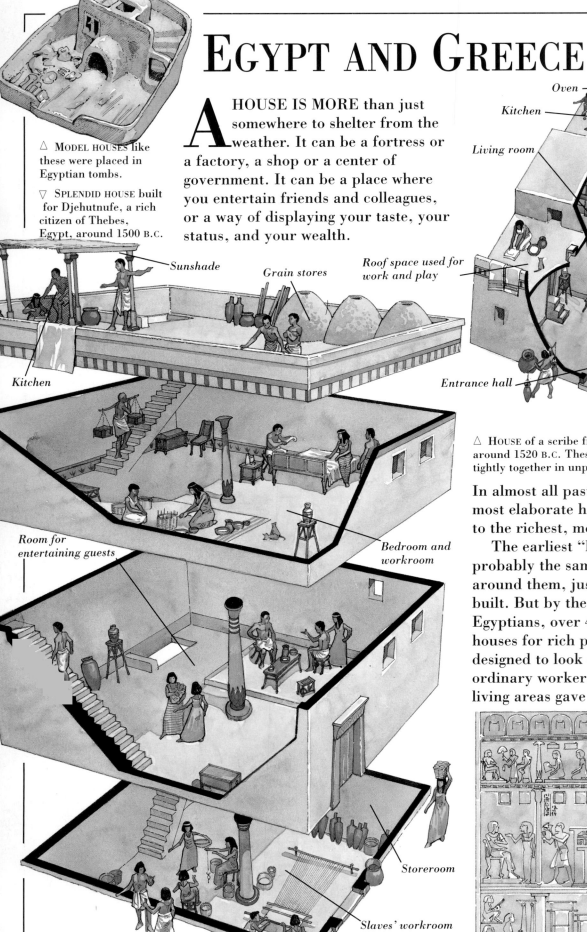

△ MODEL HOUSES like these were placed in Egyptian tombs.

▽ SPLENDID HOUSE built for Djehutnufe, a rich citizen of Thebes, Egypt, around 1500 B.C.

Sunshade

Grain stores

Kitchen

Room for entertaining guests

Bedroom and workroom

Storeroom

Slaves' workroom

△ HOUSE of a scribe from Deir El-Medina, Egypt, around 1520 B.C. These city houses were packed tightly together in unplanned streets.

In almost all past societies, the biggest, most elaborate houses have belonged to the richest, most powerful people.

The earliest "big houses" were probably the same as others all around them, just larger and better built. But by the time of the ancient Egyptians, over 4,000 years ago, houses for rich people were being designed to look different from ordinary workers' homes. Separate living areas gave privacy, away from slaves; impressive reception rooms were built for entertaining and for business use.

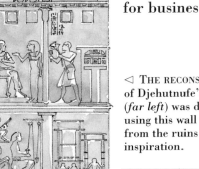

◁ THE RECONSTRUCTION of Djehutnufe's house (*far left*) was drawn using this wall painting from the ruins as inspiration.

The splendid remains of the royal palace at Knossos, on the Greek island of Crete, reveal the king's wealth and power. Houses built for rich citizens were also pleasant places to live. They were sheltered from the noise and bustle of the city by high walls, while open courtyards provided sunlight and fresh air. Separate kitchens meant people could relax in living rooms free from smoke and cooking odors.

The design of prosperous Greek homes reflected traditional beliefs and values. Each house had an altar, where prayers were said. Because well-educated Greeks believed it was shameful for women to appear in public, there were separate women's quarters, as well as a room where the men of the family could meet their male friends.

△ POTTERY MODELS of highly decorated houses, found at the town of Zakros in Crete. The patterns may have been created using paint or different-colored bricks.

△ THE PALACE of King Minos in Crete was built around 1700 B.C. Its inhabitants enjoyed great comfort and luxury. The walls were painted with beautiful frescoes; there were bathrooms, fresh running water, and lovely gardens.

▽ HOUSE at Priene, in Asia Minor, 400 B.C. It was built around an open courtyard and surrounded by a strong wall.

▷ HOUSE belonging to a wealthy family in Athens, Greece, around 400 B.C. It was built of mud bricks on a stone base, and roofed with tiles.

Women's weaving room

Tiled roof

Cooking area

Bedroom

Dining room

Strong wooden gate

Storeroom

Courtyard

Family room

Altar

9

ANCIENT ROME

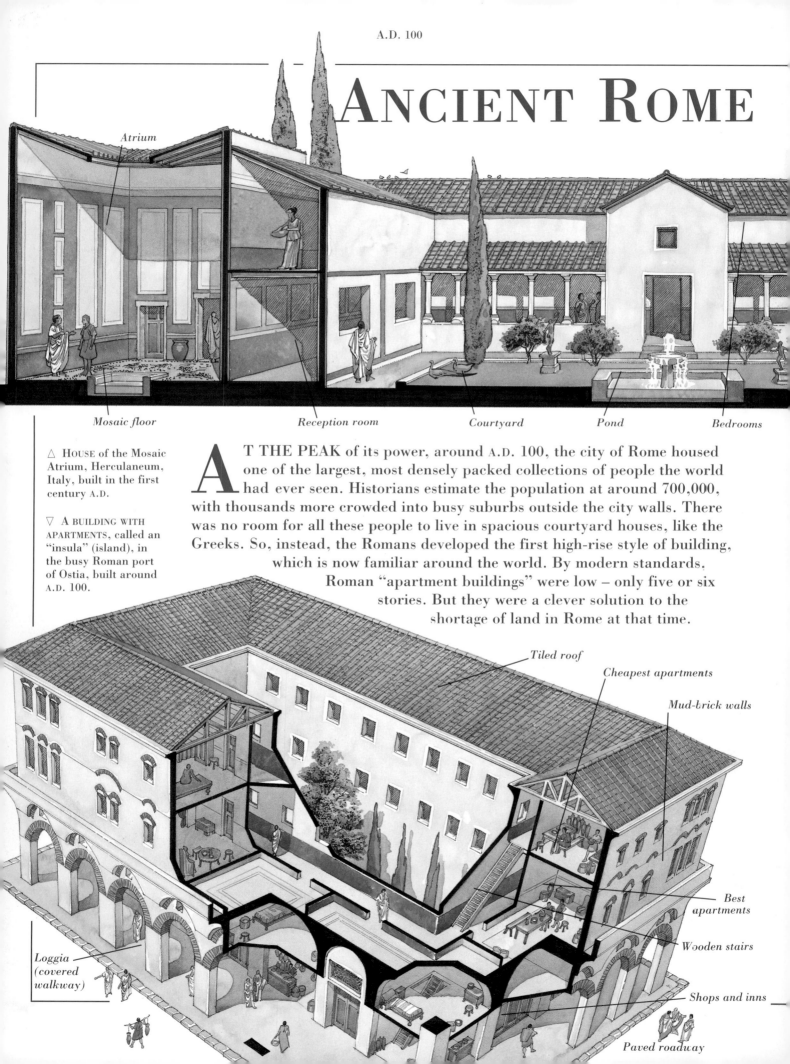

Atrium

Mosaic floor

Reception room

Courtyard

Pond

Bedrooms

△ HOUSE of the Mosaic Atrium, Herculaneum, Italy, built in the first century A.D.

▽ A BUILDING WITH APARTMENTS, called an "insula" (island), in the busy Roman port of Ostia, built around A.D. 100.

AT THE PEAK of its power, around A.D. 100, the city of Rome housed one of the largest, most densely packed collections of people the world had ever seen. Historians estimate the population at around 700,000, with thousands more crowded into busy suburbs outside the city walls. There was no room for all these people to live in spacious courtyard houses, like the Greeks. So, instead, the Romans developed the first high-rise style of building, which is now familiar around the world. By modern standards, Roman "apartment buildings" were low – only five or six stories. But they were a clever solution to the shortage of land in Rome at that time.

Tiled roof

Cheapest apartments

Mud-brick walls

Best apartments

Wooden stairs

Loggia (covered walkway)

Shops and inns

Paved roadway

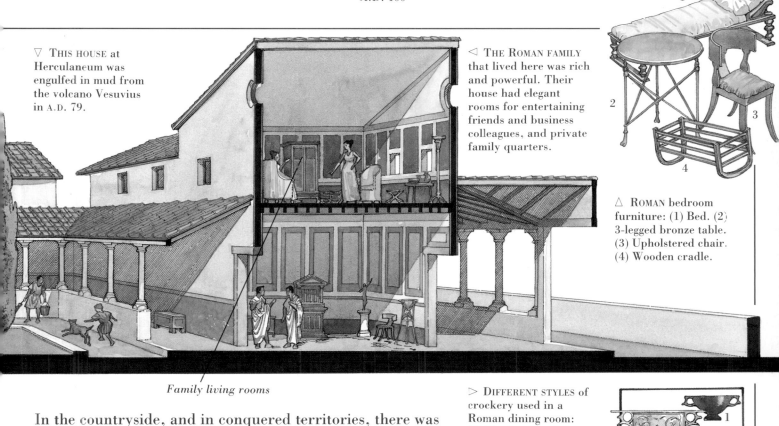

▽ THIS HOUSE at Herculaneum was engulfed in mud from the volcano Vesuvius in A.D. 79.

◁ THE ROMAN FAMILY that lived here was rich and powerful. Their house had elegant rooms for entertaining friends and business colleagues, and private family quarters.

△ ROMAN bedroom furniture: (1) Bed. (2) 3-legged bronze table. (3) Upholstered chair. (4) Wooden cradle.

Family living rooms

In the countryside, and in conquered territories, there was more space. Emperors built palaces while rich farmers and government officials built "villas," or country houses, at the center of productive estates. Villas varied; one might be a comfortable home, another a busy working farmhouse. The wealthy families who built villas had influence and could command respect. They owned the land and the slaves who farmed it. They were the leaders of local society and had links with the government in Rome.

▷ DIFFERENT STYLES of crockery used in a Roman dining room: (1) Black painted pottery cup. (2) Silver drinking vessel. (3) Red painted pottery.

▽ PALACE built for the Roman emperor Diocletian at Split, in Croatia, A.D. 300.

Main entrance

Strong outer walls

Stables and barracks for guards

Emperor's mausoleum

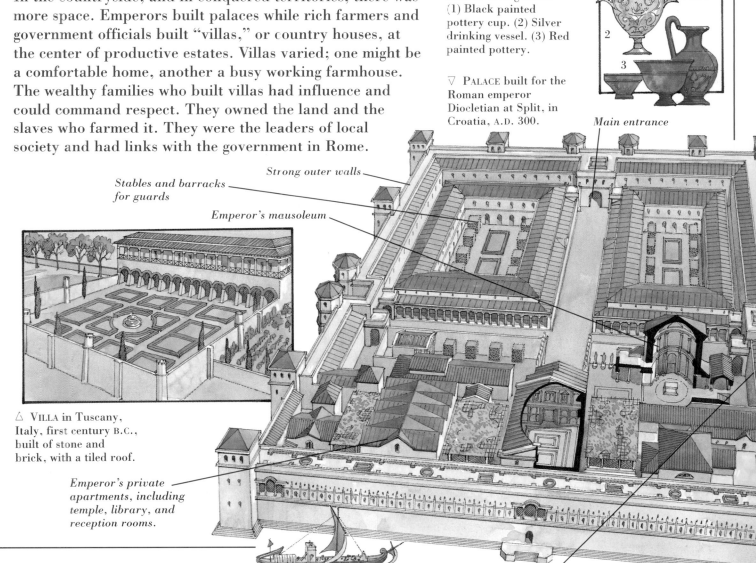

△ VILLA in Tuscany, Italy, first century B.C., built of stone and brick, with a tiled roof.

Emperor's private apartments, including temple, library, and reception rooms.

Adriatic Sea

Women's quarters

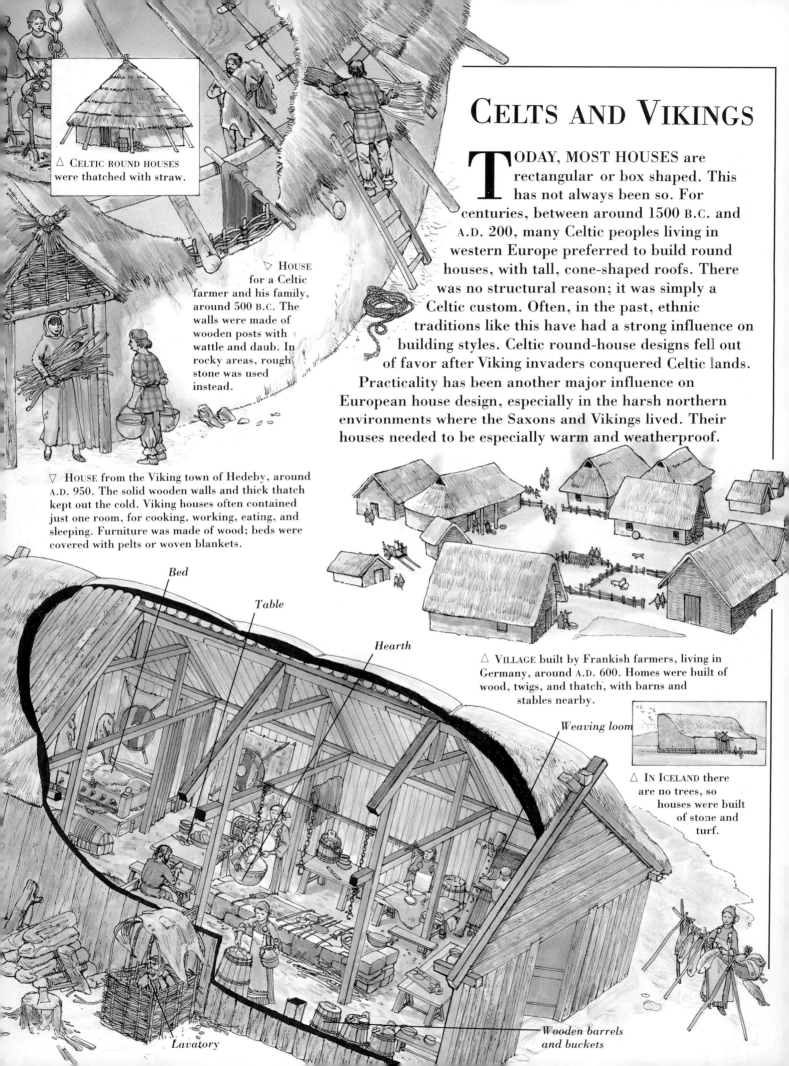

△ CELTIC ROUND HOUSES were thatched with straw.

CELTS AND VIKINGS

TODAY, MOST HOUSES are rectangular or box shaped. This has not always been so. For centuries, between around 1500 B.C. and A.D. 200, many Celtic peoples living in western Europe preferred to build round houses, with tall, cone-shaped roofs. There was no structural reason; it was simply a Celtic custom. Often, in the past, ethnic traditions like this have had a strong influence on building styles. Celtic round-house designs fell out of favor after Viking invaders conquered Celtic lands. Practicality has been another major influence on European house design, especially in the harsh northern environments where the Saxons and Vikings lived. Their houses needed to be especially warm and weatherproof.

▽ HOUSE for a Celtic farmer and his family, around 500 B.C. The walls were made of wooden posts with wattle and daub. In rocky areas, rough stone was used instead.

▽ HOUSE from the Viking town of Hedeby, around A.D. 950. The solid wooden walls and thick thatch kept out the cold. Viking houses often contained just one room, for cooking, working, eating, and sleeping. Furniture was made of wood; beds were covered with pelts or woven blankets.

Bed

Table

Hearth

△ VILLAGE built by Frankish farmers, living in Germany, around A.D. 600. Homes were built of wood, twigs, and thatch, with barns and stables nearby.

Weaving loom

△ IN ICELAND there are no trees, so houses were built of stone and turf.

Lavatory

Wooden barrels and buckets

MIDDLE AGES

▽ MANOR HOUSE belonging to a Norman lord, in England, 1200. It was built of stone and roofed with slate.

▽ UNUSUALLY LARGE stone-built house owned by a rich English wool merchant, around 1380.

Thick outer walls

Courtyard

Grooves in roof to catch rainwater

▷ COURTYARD HOUSE built for a Muslim family in southern Spain, around 1300. The flat roofs provided extra living space.

Entrance

▽ TIMBER-FRAMED hall house, around 1400. Wealthy farmers in lowland England lived in homes like this.

Living room

Bedroom

ALTHOUGH Celtic, Saxon, and Viking peoples chose different designs for their houses, the materials they used to build them – rough stone and thatch, or timber with lath and plaster – were very similar. In much of Europe, ordinary people's houses continued to be built like this throughout the Middle Ages. Repairs were a constant problem, as thatched roofs and lath and plaster walls needed replacing after about 30 years. During the Middle Ages, ordinary people's houses began to be divided into separate areas: a hall for receiving guests, a "solar" as a family room, and areas for working.

Because ordinary medieval houses were so fragile, hardly any survive today. Those that are still standing were built for wealthy families, who could afford better timber (and plenty of it) or expensive stone walls and roofs of slate or tiles.

▽ MEDIEVAL TOWN HOUSES tightly packed together inside an ancient Roman amphitheater at Arles, southern France. The strong Roman walls defended this unusual medieval town.

Upper solar

Parlor

Entrance

Hall – open to roof

MEDIEVAL CASTLES

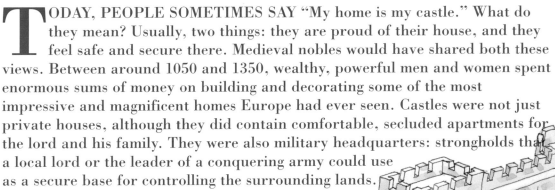

TODAY, PEOPLE SOMETIMES SAY "My home is my castle." What do they mean? Usually, two things: they are proud of their house, and they feel safe and secure there. Medieval nobles would have shared both these views. Between around 1050 and 1350, wealthy, powerful men and women spent enormous sums of money on building and decorating some of the most impressive and magnificent homes Europe had ever seen. Castles were not just private houses, although they did contain comfortable, secluded apartments for the lord and his family. They were also military headquarters: strongholds that a local lord or the leader of a conquering army could use as a secure base for controlling the surrounding lands.

△ EARLY CASTLES were built of wood, on top of an artificial mound, or "motte." They were surrounded by a strong wooden stockade called a "bailey."

△ BY THE THIRTEENTH CENTURY, castles were built of stone. They were built on sites that were difficult to reach, which made them easier to defend.

Practice yard for soldiers

Stables

Cookhouse

Outer bailey

Barn

Pigsties

Dovecote

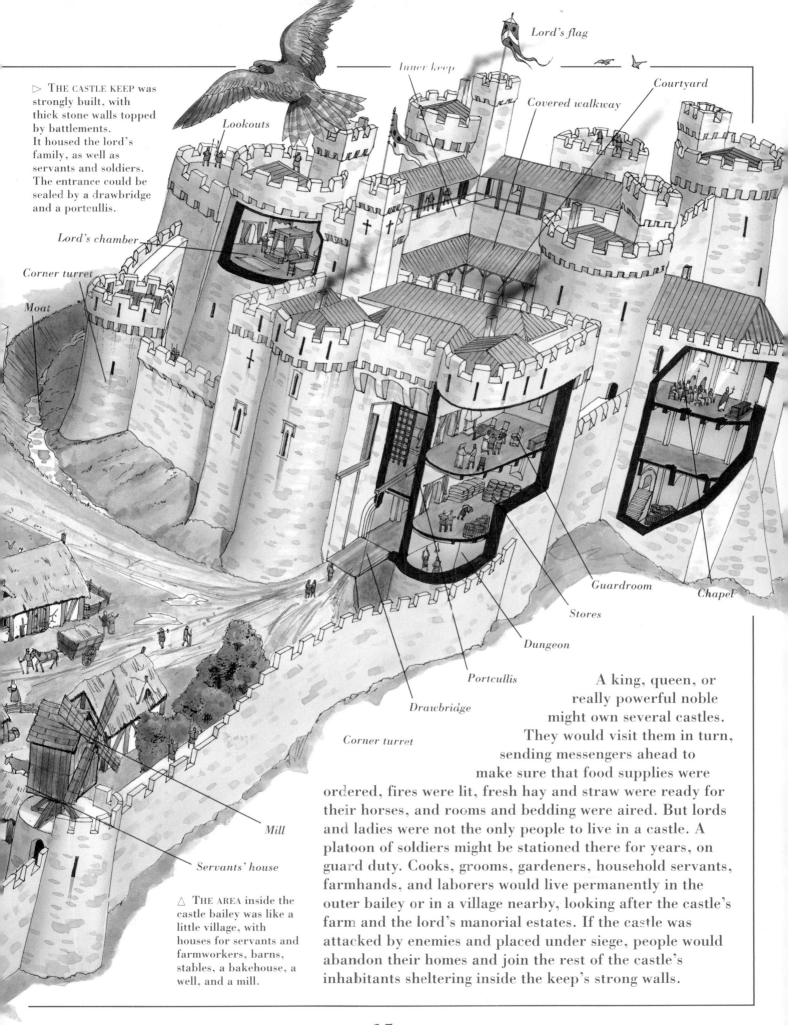

▷ THE CASTLE KEEP was strongly built, with thick stone walls topped by battlements. It housed the lord's family, as well as servants and soldiers. The entrance could be sealed by a drawbridge and a portcullis.

Lord's flag

Inner keep

Courtyard

Covered walkway

Lookouts

Lord's chamber

Corner turret

Moat

Guardroom

Chapel

Stores

Dungeon

Portcullis

Drawbridge

Corner turret

Mill

Servants' house

△ THE AREA inside the castle bailey was like a little village, with houses for servants and farmworkers, barns, stables, a bakehouse, a well, and a mill.

A king, queen, or really powerful noble might own several castles. They would visit them in turn, sending messengers ahead to make sure that food supplies were ordered, fires were lit, fresh hay and straw were ready for their horses, and rooms and bedding were aired. But lords and ladies were not the only people to live in a castle. A platoon of soldiers might be stationed there for years, on guard duty. Cooks, grooms, gardeners, household servants, farmhands, and laborers would live permanently in the outer bailey or in a village nearby, looking after the castle's farm and the lord's manorial estates. If the castle was attacked by enemies and placed under siege, people would abandon their homes and join the rest of the castle's inhabitants sheltering inside the keep's strong walls.

HOT AND COLD

Tightly-packed earth

◁ TRADITIONAL WINTER HOUSE built by people from the Bering Sea Inuit Nation. Rooms were partly underground, with low wooden walls and a wooden roof covered with earth. Grass mats provided extra insulation from the bitter Arctic cold. Houses like these were lived in mainly by women and children; men built a separate house, called a "qasgiq," for themselves nearby.

Bench for sleeping

Entrance

Logs

Ground level

SURPRISINGLY, both where it is very hot and where it is very cold people need similar houses – ones that are very well insulated. The insulation protects their homes from extreme conditions, and keeps the temperature inside as steady and comfortable as possible. Traditional materials for insulation included thatch, brushwood, and straw. Soil was also a useful barrier. In freezing Arctic lands, Inuit peoples built underground homes protected by a thick layer of earth. There were no windows, and the door was sheltered by a covered tunnel. In tropical Africa, traditional houses were also made of earth – often, mud bricks – with thick walls and roofs. In the southwestern deserts of America, Native peoples built homes underground or in deep canyons, for protection from winter snow and summer sun.

▽ TRADITIONAL WOODEN HOUSE made by people of the Sitka Native American Nation, in Alaska. The house is decorated with carved faces and other designs, recording famous ancestors of the family living there.

△ MUD-BRICK COURTYARD houses built to provide shelter from extreme dry heat in Jenne, Nigeria – almost 1,565 miles (2,500 km) from the sea.

△ FELT for a ger is made from wool fibers, dampened, rolled, and compressed.

△ GER WALLS consist of a "khana," made of crisscross willow branches tied together.

△ GER ROOF POLES are held in place by a central "crown," made of curved wood.

△ ROOF CROWNS are held in place by wooden uprights. The doorframe is also made of wood.

△ THE CRISSCROSS WALLS of the ger are kept from collapsing by a woven tension band.

△ GER DOORS are single- or double-layered (for warmth) or covered with a decorated felt flap.

▽ MONGOLIAN TENT, or "ger," made of layers of thick woolen felt stretched over a framework of light wooden poles. Mongol homes have followed this traditional design for centuries.

▽ TENT of cotton fabric and curved wood supports made by the Hammunat people, who live in the Sahara desert in Africa.

S O FAR IN THIS BOOK, we have looked at houses built by people living mainly in one place. But in some countries, a settled lifestyle was not possible. People were – and still are – nomads, traveling to hunt animals for food, or to find grazing for their animals. Many nomads live in homes similar to tents, built of cloth or skins stretched over a collapsible, portable framework of light wooden poles. Even though nomad homes are not permanent, they are skillfully made and often beautifully decorated. Unlike many other forms of building, making these "mobile homes" is very often women's work.

Tipi cover

▽ CLEANING a buffalo skin to make a tipi.

◁ NATIVE AMERICAN nations in the Great Plains lived in tipis made of buffalo skin while they traveled in search of wild animals to hunt for food. Tipis were decorated with patterns recording their owner's status or magical skills.

△ THE PUEBLO (village) of Mesa Verde in Colorado, built by the Anasazi Nation in the shelter of towering cliffs. Houses and kivas (underground meeting rooms) were made of stone.

Wooden ladder

Cliff face

Stone house

Entrance to kiva

Flat roof provides workspace

EARLY AMERICA

FOR MANY NATIVE PEOPLES in the southwestern United States, the special collection of buildings where they lived also formed their community. They were members of "pueblo" nations, sharing groups of houses joined together in a single, jumbled block, linked by steps and trackways. In homes like these, neighbors were not only next door, but above and below, as well. It is not surprising that strong, protective community loyalties developed. Women celebrated this solidarity through working together, grinding maize and baking bread, and in their poems and songs. Men and boys celebrated it with secret ceremonies, held in underground rooms called "kivas" built at the heart of each pueblo village.

▽ HOUSE from the Inca city of Machu Picchu, Peru, around 1450. Stones for the walls were chipped and smoothed by hand, to fit closely together. The roof was thatched.

▽ TRADITIONAL HOGAN (earth house) made by Navaho people, who lived in the harsh climate of the American Southwest. A wooden frame was covered with earth, to give insulation.

▽ NATIVE AMERICAN VILLAGE, Florida, around 1600. Houses were built of timber, thatched with leaves, and surrounded by a strong timber stockade.

△ NATIVE AMERICAN HOUSE from Virginia, around 1600, made of a wooden frame covered with woven mats.

△ AZTEC HOME in Mexico, around 1450, built of sun-dried mud bricks and thatched with reeds. The walls were painted with limewash, to waterproof them.

▽ TWO VIEWS of a traditional Native American pueblo in New Mexico. Houses were built close together in multistory terraces. Upper floors were reached by ladders.

Pueblos – which still exist – are remarkable for the way in which their architecture mirrors the feelings of the people who live there. Other early American homes were remarkable, too – making the best possible use of the local environment, allowing Native peoples to survive. Traditionally, houses in the high Andes mountains of Peru were built of skillfully shaped stone; they could survive earthquakes that destroy the modern brick buildings of today. In the dense forests of Florida and Virginia, there were no building stones; so walls, roofs, and even statues of the gods were all made from different parts of trees. In Mexico, the Aztecs created vegetable gardens ("chinampas") on land reclaimed from vast lakes and built farmhouses of dried lake mud.

◁ MOHAWK Native American village, New York State, 1750.

RENAISSANCE EUROPE

B Y THE FIFTEENTH CENTURY, the families of many merchants and craftsmen in European towns were used to living "above the shop." Houses were designed to combine working space with living space; there was usually room for storing and selling goods, too. The whole family worked together in a business. Craftsmen wove cloth, or produced fine leather goods, metalwork, or jewelry. Merchants arranged complicated international deals, buying and selling imported luxuries such as silks, sugar, and spices. Men trained their sons and apprentices – who lived with the family – in all their "trade secrets." Women and girls served customers and kept accounts, as well as organized servants, arranged meals, and generally ran the household. These urban working houses were not all the same. Some were small and cramped, while others were large and spacious. They ranged from poor craftworkers' cottages in England to magnificent timber-framed town houses belonging to merchants in Germany, and fine stone palazzi (palaces) built for Italian entrepreneurs (businessmen who took risks to develop new kinds of companies).

△ TIMBER-FRAMED HOUSE built for a merchant in Nuremberg, Germany, fifteenth century.

△ TIMBER-FRAMED HOUSES built for craftsmen (weavers) in the small town of Lavenham, Suffolk, around 1490.

△ STONE HOUSE built for a wealthy Italian merchant in Venice, Italy, around 1490.

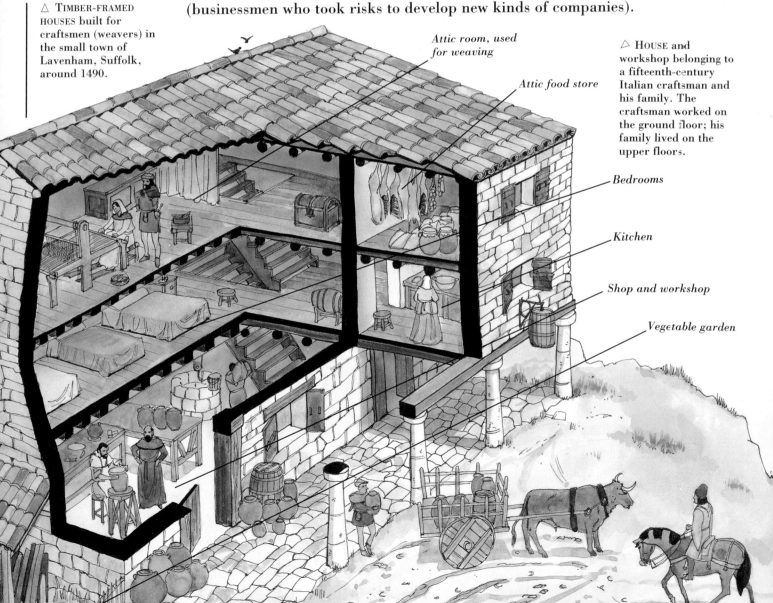

Attic room, used for weaving

Attic food store

△ HOUSE and workshop belonging to a fifteenth-century Italian craftsman and his family. The craftsman worked on the ground floor; his family lived on the upper floors.

Bedrooms

Kitchen

Shop and workshop

Vegetable garden

During the Renaissance centuries, trade prospered and populations grew. Leading commercial families became very rich. To advertise their business success and display the wealth they had earned, they commissioned houses (with shop and office space) in the fashionable Renaissance style. Soon, French and Italian town councils encouraged architects to design more Renaissance-style buildings to bring prestige and eager new customers to their towns.

△ WEALTHY FAMILIES could afford to build homes with separate areas for cooking (done by servants), eating, and sleeping, like this fifteenth-century Italian house. Other rooms were used for storage, offices, and a shop.

△ RENAISSANCE FURNITURE: (1) Bed with canopy. (2) Narrow wardrobe. (3) Chest for storage. (4) Chair. (5) Table.

▷ PURPOSE-BUILT BUILDING with loggia (covered walkway) and shops, plus apartments for owners and workers on the upper floors. From Lyons, France, 1540-1542. Twelve families of shopkeepers lived here.

Apartments

Loggia

Shops

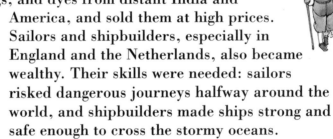

▽ INSIDE THE HOUSE of a poor worker's family in seventeenth-century Netherlands. Furniture was simple – a chair, a cupboard, and a bed. But there was a fireplace with a chimney, and glass in the window.

▷ STREET-FRONT in a prosperous city; houses along the street known as Keizersgracht, in seventeenth-century Amsterdam, in the Netherlands. Houses like these were richly furnished and very comfortable. There was still space allowed for household tasks, and for stores of goods.

NORTHERN EUROPE

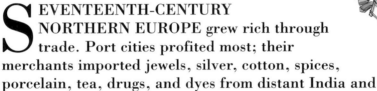

▽ TOWN HOUSE belonging to a wealthy family in Plymouth, England, early seventeenth century. In crowded cities, houses were built several stories high, to make the best use of space.

SEVENTEENTH-CENTURY NORTHERN EUROPE grew rich through trade. Port cities profited most; their merchants imported jewels, silver, cotton, spices, porcelain, tea, drugs, and dyes from distant India and America, and sold them at high prices. Sailors and shipbuilders, especially in England and the Netherlands, also became wealthy. Their skills were needed: sailors risked dangerous journeys halfway around the world, and shipbuilders made ships strong and safe enough to cross the stormy oceans.

Traditionally, town houses in northern Europe were made of a timber framework, filled in with wattle and daub, and roofed with thatch. Brick-built houses had been pioneered in coastal cities of the Baltic region during the fifteenth century. By 1600, the prosperity resulting from trade encouraged this technique to spread to the Netherlands and countries nearby. Bricks were expensive, but allowed taller, stronger structures to be built. Bricks were also fire resistant; this was important where houses were built close together. In the seventeenth century, timber-framed houses were banned in Amsterdam, because of the risk of fire.

Inside a typical brick town house, Protestant, puritan taste dictated that everything be plain but good quality, and designed to last. Northern houses may have been less elegant than comparable Italian homes, but they were probably far more cozy.

AFRICA

IN MANY PARTS OF THE WORLD, stone suitable for building is very hard to find. Even where it exists, people may not have the tools to quarry it, or the money to pay workers to carve it. But whatever the shortages – of materials or labor – men and women have developed many traditional ways of building secure, weatherproof homes. Although these traditional houses may be simple in construction, they are carefully and thoughtfully designed.

In parts of Africa, "living walls" of bushes are planted to protect villages from enemies or wild animals. Properly maintained, they are impossible to cross. In areas where the land often floods, wooden houses (which would let in water if built at ground level) are raised high on stilts. Where there is no stone and no timber either, houses are built of woven grass matting, or sun-dried mud. Decorated doors, windows, and walls are used to distinguish homes belonging to community leaders or other important people.

△ VILLAGE in Cameroon, encircled by defensive walls of spiny, poisonous plants.

▽ GINNA (house belonging to a senior priest of the Dogon people) in Mali.

◁ MABAS HOUSES from Cameroon, made from stone with thatched roofs of straw often several layers thick. Each group of houses contains a separate family.

◁ CARVED and finely decorated doorway of a traditional house, made of clay bricks, at Kano in Nigeria.

▽ HOUSES in Ganvie, Dahomey. The entire town is built on stilts above the water.

24

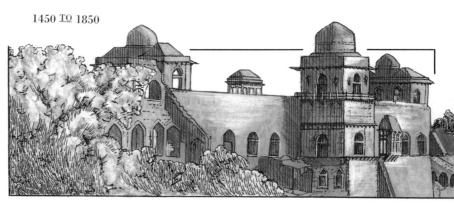

INDIA

THE SUBCONTINENT OF INDIA is a vast and varied landscape, and has proved a rich prize for conquerors for hundreds of years. Most foreign rulers of India have been influenced by the ancient civilization they found there. But they have also encouraged the spread of their own cultures, especially art, architecture, languages, and laws. As a result, India today contains many buildings from the past that were designed in a blend of local and imported styles.

This "cultural mix" is most easily seen in houses built for wealthy and powerful families. Ordinary people's homes – the majority – have been much less affected by fashions from abroad. Instead, like simple housing all over the world, their designs have been influenced by the needs and traditions of people who live there, and by the building materials available.

△ THE JAHAZ MAHAL palace built in Afghan style for the rulers of Mandu, central India, fifteenth century.

▷ TRADITIONAL village house in the north Indian state of Kashmir, 1760.

▷ PALACE built in European style for the Indian rajas (kings) of Tanjore, 1828.

△ PALACE at Amber, built around 1600 for the Rajput rulers of Kachwaha state. It was constructed from magnificently carved stone, on a dramatic, well-defended site, and was used as the main state residence until the city of Jaipur was founded in 1727.

▽ EUROPEAN-STYLE HOUSE owned by a wealthy British family in India, early nineteenth century. It was set in spacious gardens, and had cool underground rooms, used during the hot weather. Many British merchants and East India Company officials built homes like this.

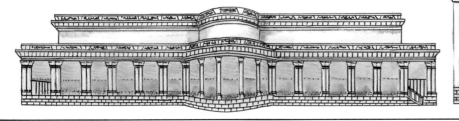

25

◁ HIMEJI CASTLE, rebuilt in 1608. The splendid keep, made of wood and plaster, was built on, and surrounded by, strong stone walls.

JAPAN

EVERY COMMUNITY, past or present, has a "secret language" of style, clearly understood by its members but puzzling to outsiders. Traditional Japanese buildings are a good example of this. They carried a very clear message about their owner's status in society. For instance, by the seventeenth century, few Japanese lords lived in the magnificent wood-and-plaster castles they built in the traditional style. Instead, they lived with their families and bodyguards in strong stone houses nearby.

▽ TRADITIONAL Japanese houses had separate buildings called "kura" for storage. This highly decorated kura dates from the late 1500s.

▽ HOUSES IN JAPAN were often built with a separate teahouse, used for ceremonial entertaining.

Teahouse

Washroom and lavatory

Kettle and fresh water

Main house

Other Japanese buildings displayed their owner's education, elegance, and refinement. The gracious tea ceremony was said to have been invented by a fifteenth-century monk, and soon became popular among people who shared his scholarly, philosophical views. It was a great compliment to your guests to invite them to your teahouse to share this ceremony in exquisite, tranquil surroundings.

CHINA

△ POTTERY MODEL, around A.D. 100, of a traditional Chinese courtyard house.

FAMILIES were the most important group in Chinese society, and Chinese homes reflected this. Houses were large enough to accommodate an entire extended family: parents, married sons and their wives, grandchildren, and great-grandchildren. Space was also provided at a family altar for the spirits of long-dead ancestors.

Chinese families lived on farms, in craft workshops, and on fishing boats. Small-scale models, buried in tombs, depict family businesses and provide information about ordinary Chinese homes that disappeared long ago.

Tomb models were made of clay, but in real life building materials depended on the locality. In the north and along rocky coasts, homes were made of brick or stone; in the southeast, where trees flourished, houses were built of wood. In central China, dwellings were carved out of "loess" – topsoil, several feet thick. Some of these artificial caves are still lived in today.

Bedroom

Living room

▽ ELEGANT eighteenth-century Chinese house, built on two stories. The outer walls were stone; inside, floors, partitions, and pillars were made of wood.

Kitchen

Courtyard

△ NINETEENTH-CENTURY village house, Hong Kong – home to a large family who worked together. Chinese village houses were built around a central courtyard. Inhabitants were guarded by a strong gate and thick walls.

△ ANOTHER pottery model from a Chinese tomb dating from the first century A.D., showing a lavatory-plus-pigsty. This arrangement was common on many farms.

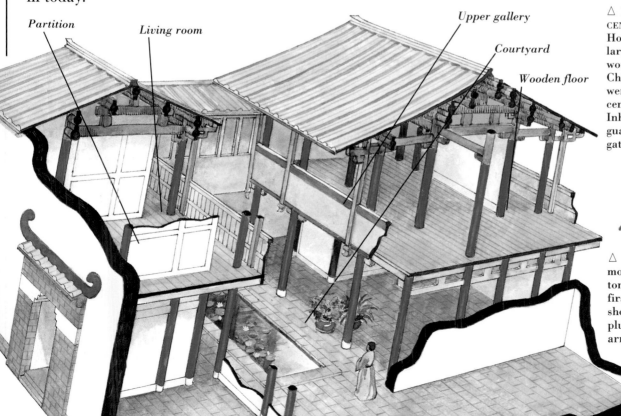

Partition

Living room

Upper gallery

Courtyard

Wooden floor

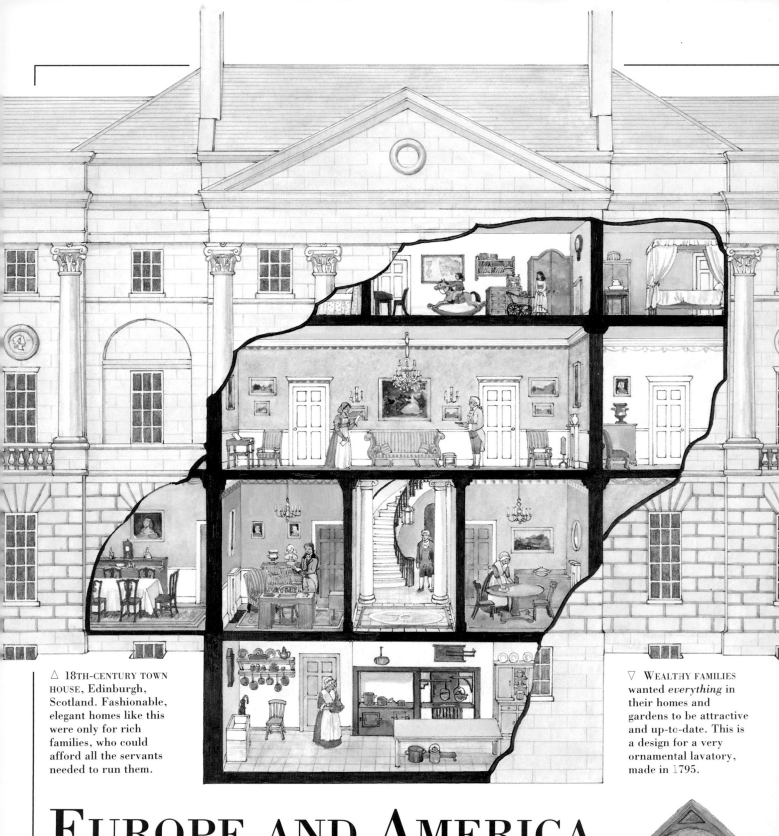

△ 18TH-CENTURY TOWN HOUSE, Edinburgh, Scotland. Fashionable, elegant homes like this were only for rich families, who could afford all the servants needed to run them.

▽ WEALTHY FAMILIES wanted *everything* in their homes and gardens to be attractive and up-to-date. This is a design for a very ornamental lavatory, made in 1795.

EUROPE AND AMERICA

SOME HISTORIANS call the eighteenth century "the peak of European civilization." Artists, writers, and composers were producing brilliant masterpieces; clothes, jewels, and furnishings were graceful and attractive. European architects such as the Adam brothers were designing houses that many people describe as the most stylish ever built, grouped in elegant terraces or large, open squares surrounding formal gardens.

△ HOW AN eighteenth-century pioneer farm developed: first, land was cleared and a log cabin was built.

△ MORE LAND was cleared and cultivated; the log cabin was enlarged and made more comfortable.

△ AS THE FARM PROSPERED, a new, two-story house was built, along with fences and barns.

△ THE FARMER now lived in a grand mansion. No trace of the original woodland remained.

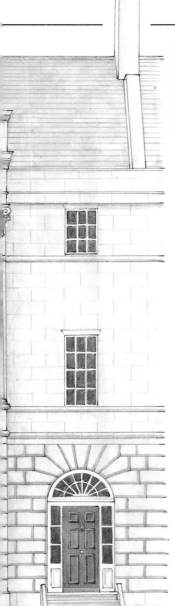

But all this could be only for the wealthy few, who depended on large numbers of servants, laborers, and craftworkers to produce the fine houses and luxury goods that they enjoyed in such high style.

For ordinary people, life was not so civilized. In the countryside, farm laborers faced poverty and the threat of starvation. Often, they could not afford to repair their leaking, ramshackle homes. In the growing industrial towns, wages were higher, but housing conditions were grim.

Many people made the brave decision to emigrate to America and start a new life there, as farmers or traders. With good luck and hard work, they might make their fortune. Through their efforts, a bold new pioneer civilization began.

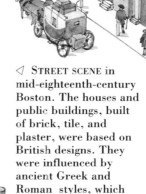

◁ STREET SCENE in mid-eighteenth-century Boston. The houses and public buildings, built of brick, tile, and plaster, were based on British designs. They were influenced by ancient Greek and Roman styles, which were fashionable in Europe.

▽ SOD HOUSE (made of slabs of turf) built by European settlers in Nebraska, c.1887. Turf was used in this way in areas where few trees grew and wood was scarce.

THE WHITE HOUSE

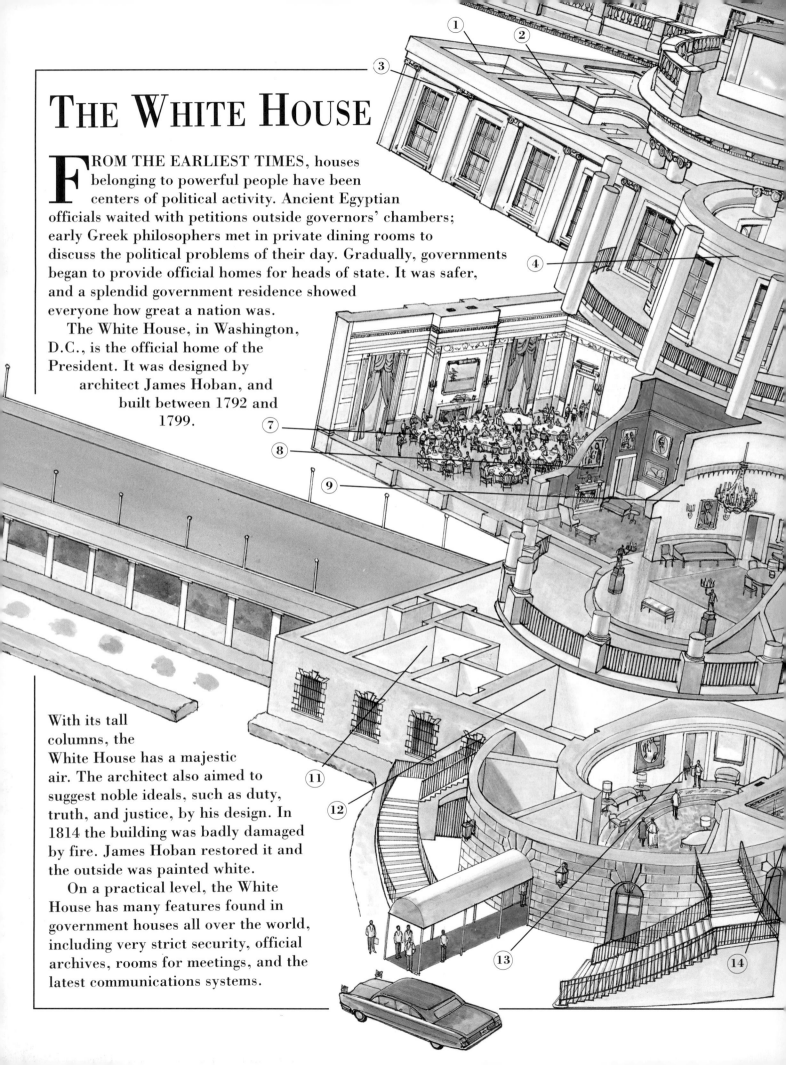

FROM THE EARLIEST TIMES, houses belonging to powerful people have been centers of political activity. Ancient Egyptian officials waited with petitions outside governors' chambers; early Greek philosophers met in private dining rooms to discuss the political problems of their day. Gradually, governments began to provide official homes for heads of state. It was safer, and a splendid government residence showed everyone how great a nation was.

The White House, in Washington, D.C., is the official home of the President. It was designed by architect James Hoban, and built between 1792 and 1799.

With its tall columns, the White House has a majestic air. The architect also aimed to suggest noble ideals, such as duty, truth, and justice, by his design. In 1814 the building was badly damaged by fire. James Hoban restored it and the outside was painted white.

On a practical level, the White House has many features found in government houses all over the world, including very strict security, official archives, rooms for meetings, and the latest communications systems.

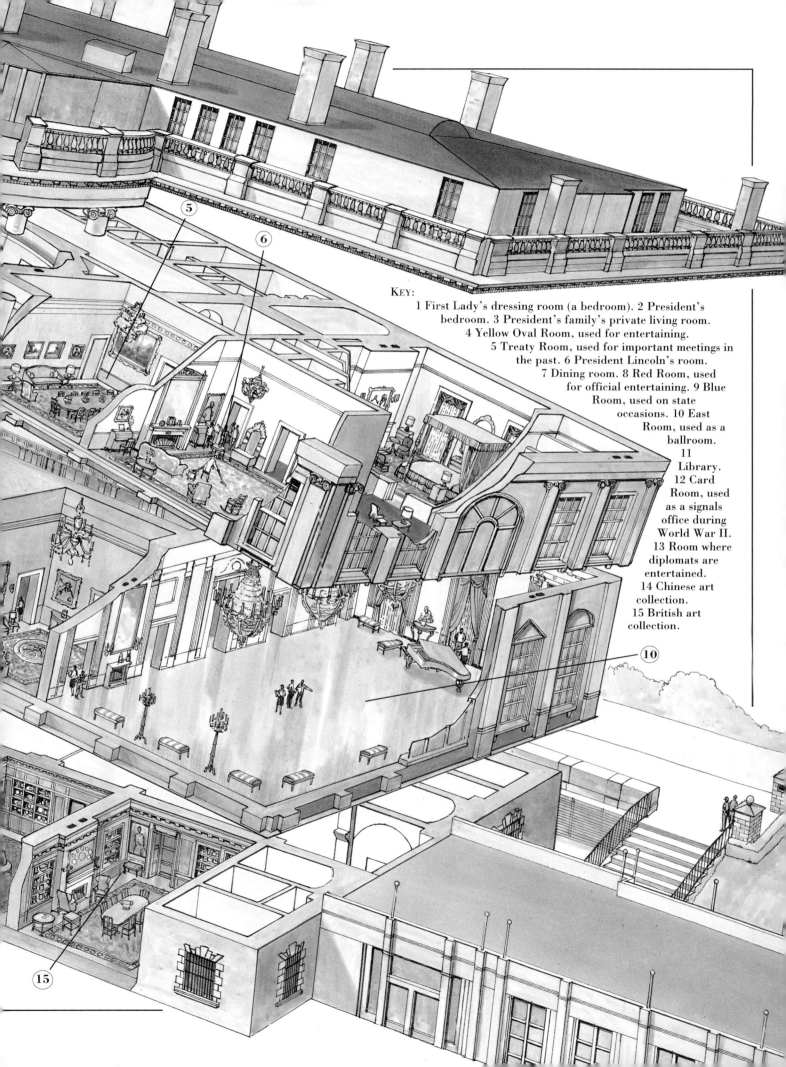

KEY:

1 First Lady's dressing room (a bedroom). 2 President's bedroom. 3 President's family's private living room. 4 Yellow Oval Room, used for entertaining. 5 Treaty Room, used for important meetings in the past. 6 President Lincoln's room. 7 Dining room. 8 Red Room, used for official entertaining. 9 Blue Room, used on state occasions. 10 East Room, used as a ballroom. 11 Library. 12 Card Room, used as a signals office during World War II. 13 Room where diplomats are entertained. 14 Chinese art collection. 15 British art collection.

WORKERS' HOMES

THE WEALTHY PEOPLE who built fine houses in Europe and America during the eighteenth century admired the cottages they could see from their coach windows as they traveled through the countryside. They called them charming and quaint. But what were these homes really like to live in? Today, some historians have termed them rural slums. Country cottages were mostly poorly built, often in need of repairs, and almost always damp, dark, and overcrowded. Furniture was sparse and shabby; there might be one bed, a table, and a few chairs. Rooms were heated by an open fire burning wood or coal. A few skilled craftworkers might be able to buy their own home, but most cottages were rented from a rich farmer or landlord. A single dwelling might be divided between several families, too poor to afford a whole house to themselves. Farm wages were very low, and farmwork was available for only part of the year. So, to avoid starvation, families had to find extra work.

△ ORDINARY PEOPLE could afford only smelly tallow (sheep's fat) candles or rush lamps. Both gave a dim, flickering light, but enabled families to work after dark.

△ THIS seventeenth-century French peasant family have brought some of their simple furniture outdoors, while selling bread and beer.

△ INSIDE a prosperous craftworker's home in Germany, 1823. The family, including all the children, are making straw hats to sell.

▽ THIS NINETEENTH-CENTURY German weaver's loom occupies almost all the space in his cottage. He has just a single room for working, eating, and sleeping.

In towns, conditions were not much better. During the nineteenth century, millions of new homes were built to house factory workers in the rapidly growing industrial cities of Europe and America. But they were often of a very low standard. Builders and developers were more interested in cramming the largest number of people into the smallest space – that way, they got more rent – than in providing comfortable, healthy homes where families could live.

△ TRADITIONAL laborer's cottage, County Cork, Ireland. It was built of rough stone and roofed with slabs of turf.

▽ WORKERS' HOUSING, close to a busy railroad line, London, 1870s. Terraced houses like these provided privacy for individual families, but were often damp, grimy, and infested with bugs and fleas.

▽ NINETEENTH-CENTURY HOUSE in northern Russia, built of thick timber logs with a wooden plank roof. The walls were lined with more timber, to keep out the bitter winter cold.

▽ WOODEN BARRACK-TYPE BUILDING built to house French- Canadian immigrants in Massachusetts, around 1900. Families came from Canada seeking work in America's growing industrial towns. Their lives could be grim, at work and in living quarters like these.

△ SOME OF THE SERVANTS needed to run a country estate.
1 Butler.
2 House steward.
3 Groom of the chambers.
4 Valet.
5 Lady's maid.
6 Housekeeper.
7 Nanny.
8 Footman.
9 Housemaid.
10 Kitchen maid.
11 Tweenies.
12 Hallboy or "Boots."
13 Estate manager.
14 Gamekeeper.
15 Carpenter.
16 Blacksmith.
17 Groom.
18 Farm laborers.
19 Kennel boys.
20 Coachman.

STATELY HOMES

LIKE MEDIEVAL CASTLES BEFORE THEM, the great European country houses of the eighteenth and nineteenth centuries were separate, almost self-contained, worlds. For the owner, a large estate with a splendid house meant pride, power, and responsibility. For tenants and ordinary people living nearby, a big house and its fields, farms, gardens, and workshops meant the chance of a secure job, and (possibly) someone to turn to for help when times were bad. But it also meant fitting in with the political views or personal eccentricities of the owner and his family. Many whims were harmless – one duke called all his footmen "William" whatever their real names. But, for the servants, they were humiliating, too.

Building and maintaining a big house cost an enormous amount of money. Wages alone might take almost half of an owner's income. Senior servants were well paid; a butler might earn $200 a year (top craftsman's wages) in the mid-nineteenth century, plus board and lodging. Decorations and furniture in the grand manner – staterooms for visitors, luxurious private apartments, a library, a picture gallery, and a huge kitchen – brought many owners close to bankruptcy.

▷ A NINETEENTH-CENTURY COUNTRY HOUSE and its estate buildings, at Erddig, in Wales. Estates like these dominated the countryside for miles around. Their owners were major employers. Although they aimed to use mainly their own produce – from their farms and their vegetable gardens – they were also the most important customers of many local businesses.

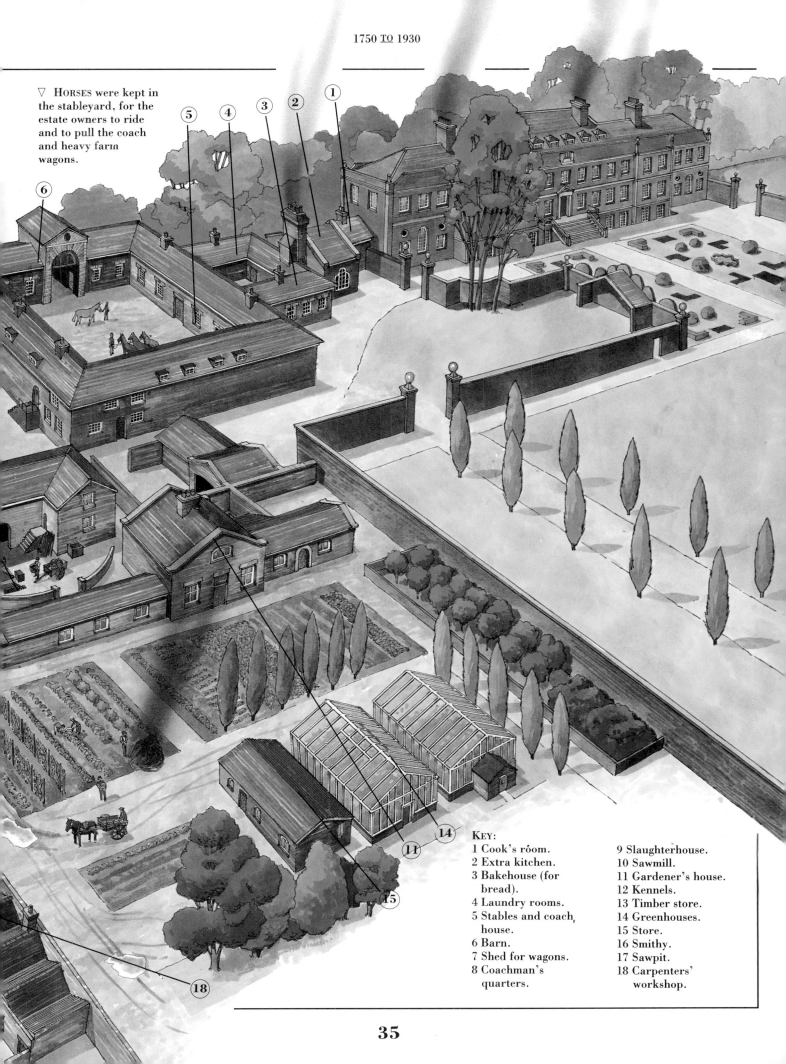

▽ HORSES were kept in the stableyard, for the estate owners to ride and to pull the coach and heavy farm wagons.

KEY:
1 Cook's room.
2 Extra kitchen.
3 Bakehouse (for bread).
4 Laundry rooms.
5 Stables and coach house.
6 Barn.
7 Shed for wagons.
8 Coachman's quarters.
9 Slaughterhouse.
10 Sawmill.
11 Gardener's house.
12 Kennels.
13 Timber store.
14 Greenhouses.
15 Store.
16 Smithy.
17 Sawpit.
18 Carpenters' workshop.

△ THE RED HOUSE, Kent, England. Designed in 1859 by the architect Philip Webb for the famous arts and crafts designer, William Morris.

▽ COMFORTABLE suburban houses, each with a garden, at Bedford Park, London. Designed by the architect Richard Norman Shaw and his partners in 1875.

SUBURBAN STYLE

FOR CENTURIES, no one lived in a city unless they had to. Cities were crowded, dirty, and unhealthy. City dwellers were usually desperate (mostly homeless and unemployed), rich merchants, or adventurers seeking their fortune. Wealthy people might visit a city – to go shopping, to take part in politics, or to enjoy fashionable entertainments - but they soon escaped with relief to the fresh air and clean surroundings of their country homes.

During the nineteenth century, cities in Europe and the United States grew rapidly, but for the majority of inhabitants, conditions did not improve. Slum housing and polluted water led to dangerous epidemics. There was violence, drunkenness, and crime. People who could afford it moved out to one of the new suburbs, where houses were well built, the air was clean, and there was piped water and good drainage.

▽ SHERMAN HOUSE, Newport, Connecticut, 1880s. Designed as a copy of traditional seventeenth-century English houses, and influenced by The Red House and Bedford Park (above).

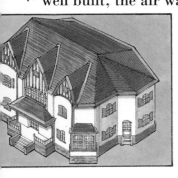

△ BLOEMENWERF VILLA, Brussels, Belgium. Built in 1896 in the glamorous continental art nouveau style, by artist and architect Henry van der Velde. The villa's design was also influenced by Dutch seventeenth-century houses (see pages 22-23.)

▷ A RESTRAINED English interpretation of the arts and crafts style – The Orchard, Chorley Wood, England, 1900.

Today, the word suburban is often used to mean "dull and boring," but between around 1870 and 1930 the suburbs were trendsetters in style. For the first time, famous, professional architects concerned themselves with designing homes for people who were not rich and famous. (Before, homes were built by local builders.) These new suburban homes displayed a fanciful mixture of design details – such as mock timber decoration – but the houses themselves were comfortable and pleasant to live in. Also for the first time, architects were employed by only moderately well-off patrons – artists, bankers, and businesspeople – to build fashionable individual houses, in town and country, in the latest styles.

△ THE ORCHARD was designed by architect C.F.A. Voysey as his own home. He aimed at – and achieved – a pure, simple, "honest" design.

▽ THE PALAIS STOCKLET, Brussels, Belgium, built for a wealthy banker between 1905-11. It was constructed of marble and bronze, and decorated with fine sculptures.

△ MOCK TUDOR brick and timber house, Britain, 1930s. Millions of homes like these were built for middle-class families in the suburbs.

◁ STEEL-FRAMED Schröder-Schräder House, Utrecht, Netherlands.

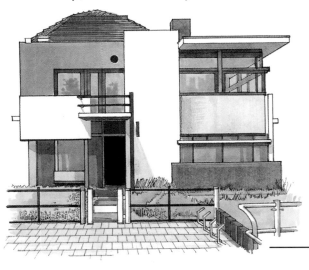

△ FALLINGWATER, Bear Run, Pennsylvania. A striking concrete house on a dramatic site above a waterfall, designed in 1936 by architect Frank Lloyd Wright. The wide picture windows make the most of the view.

HIGH-RISE

SUBURBS WERE ONE WAY of improving housing for city dwellers. But they had two major drawbacks: they used a lot of land, and people who lived in them had to travel to work. Nevertheless, they remained popular in Britain and the United States, replacing grim, unsafe tenements for almost 100 years.

In Europe, architects tried different solutions to the problem of finding space for city housing. Sometimes traditional houses were just made taller. But engineering reasons limited these buildings to about six stories high. Sometimes, commercial zones were used for housing: new buildings combined attractive street-level shops with spacious apartments on upper floors. A few architects used wild, imaginative decoration to make crowded apartments seem "friendly" and inviting. At the same time, they experimented with new materials (concrete and steel) and with new methods of construction, such as prefabrication.

From the 1930s, architects inspired by American hotel and office skyscrapers designed massive, high-rise towers. At first, they were welcomed as exciting "vertical streets," but today we know that some people find them lonely and frightening to live in.

△ SECTION of an apartment complex, Italy, 1910. The land once occupied by one medium-sized house now provided living space for several families.

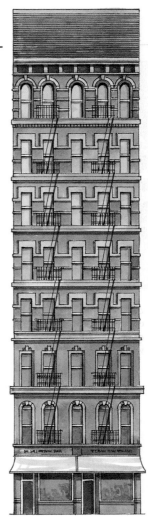

△ TENEMENTS (working-class apartments), New York, late nineteenth century. Apartments like this often had poor ventilation and few toilets.

◁ MAJOLICA HOUSE, Vienna, Austria, c.1900. Elaborately decorated apartments built above shops.

▽ LUXURY BUILDING, with windows and balconies facing a park, Paris, France, 1902-3.

◁ THE CASA MILÁ, in Barcelona, Spain, designed by Antoni Gaudí, 1905-10.

△ FOR THE CASA MILÁ, Gaudí used exaggerated, curving walls and fantastically shaped chimneys to create an unusual, exciting apartment building. It was built of concrete.

△ HIGHPOINT I, a spacious luxury apartment building in an exclusive district of London, designed by a pioneering group of architects known as "Tecton" in 1933.

◁ HOUSING PROJECTS with tower and slab buildings, plus smaller, lower buildings, designed between 1956-1960 to house 9,500 people at Roehampton, London.

◁ THE UNITÉ D'HABITATION ("one-place living") complex, Marseilles, France, designed by architect Le Corbusier, 1946-52. Built of concrete and glass, it was planned as a self-contained community. It has shops, offices, cafes, studios, workshops, meeting places, a community center, a theater, a nursery, and a gym, as well as apartments for 1,600 people.

▷ APARTMENT COMPLEX Habitat 67, Montreal, Canada. Designed by architect Moshe Safdie. Each apartment was pre-fabricated, then lifted into place – a very expensive way of building.

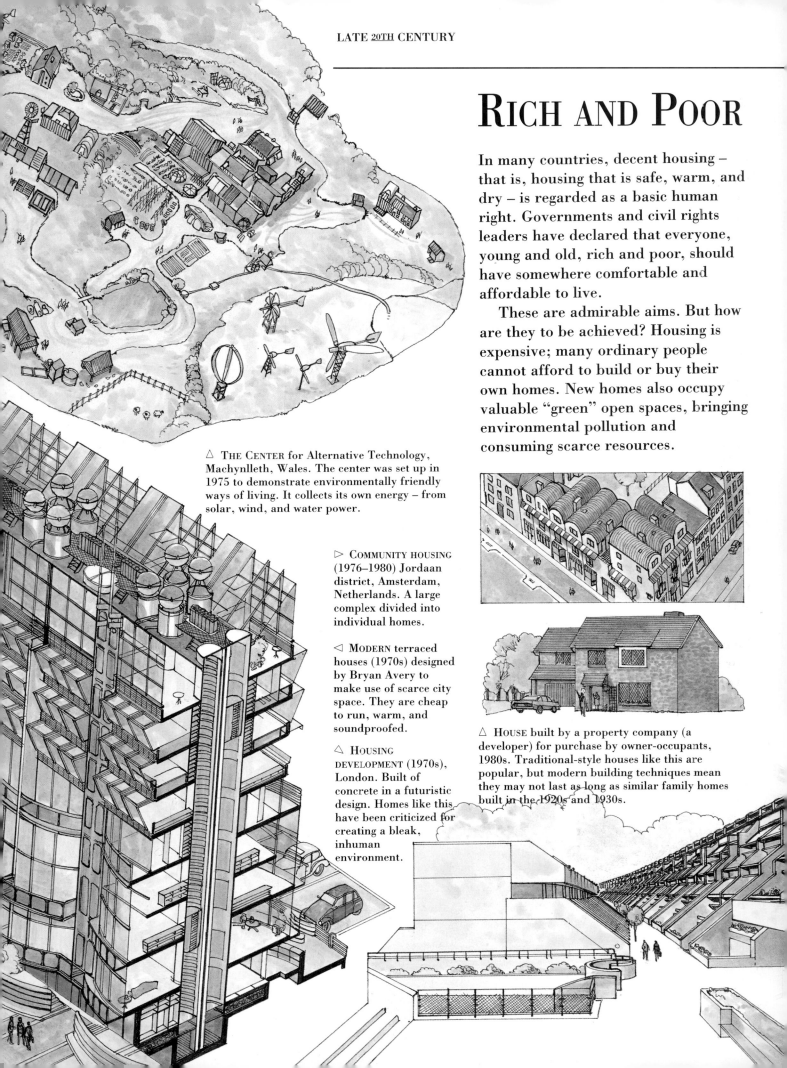

RICH AND POOR

In many countries, decent housing – that is, housing that is safe, warm, and dry – is regarded as a basic human right. Governments and civil rights leaders have declared that everyone, young and old, rich and poor, should have somewhere comfortable and affordable to live.

These are admirable aims. But how are they to be achieved? Housing is expensive; many ordinary people cannot afford to build or buy their own homes. New homes also occupy valuable "green" open spaces, bringing environmental pollution and consuming scarce resources.

△ THE CENTER for Alternative Technology, Machynlleth, Wales. The center was set up in 1975 to demonstrate environmentally friendly ways of living. It collects its own energy – from solar, wind, and water power.

▷ COMMUNITY HOUSING (1976–1980) Jordaan district, Amsterdam, Netherlands. A large complex divided into individual homes.

◁ MODERN terraced houses (1970s) designed by Bryan Avery to make use of scarce city space. They are cheap to run, warm, and soundproofed.

△ HOUSING DEVELOPMENT (1970s), London. Built of concrete in a futuristic design. Homes like this have been criticized for creating a bleak, inhuman environment.

△ HOUSE built by a property company (a developer) for purchase by owner-occupants, 1980s. Traditional-style houses like this are popular, but modern building techniques mean they may not last as long as similar family homes built in the 1920s and 1930s.

Planners and politicians have suggested several solutions to these problems. Environmentalists have designed low-energy homes, built of cheap, renewable resources, well insulated (to save heat loss) and able to trap natural energy from sun, wind, or water. National and local governments have sponsored public housing programs, building estates of homes for ordinary people to rent.

▷ MILLIONS of people in many lands still live in homes like this shantytown on the outskirts of a big city.

▷ HOUSES in shanty-towns are built of any materials that can be found nearby: scrap metal, plastic sheeting, and oddments of lumber. There are usually no safe gas or electricity supplies, no plumbing or toilets.

In wealthy countries, banks and building societies lend money to help working people buy their own homes. Community groups join together to create neighborhood programs, where local people can advise the architects.

Sadly, these options are not available to everyone. In many countries, such as Russia and China, there is a serious housing shortage. In parts of Asia, Africa, and South America, jobs are scarce and wages are low, so families leave their villages and travel to cities in search of work. The only homes they can find are in shantytowns. Even in wealthy countries, there are people living in poor conditions.

▽ HOMELESS PEOPLE seek shelter in "cardboard cities," made of old boxes and packing cases, huddled under bridges, railroad embankments, or in doorways. Poor conditions like these can lead to disease and even to death.

THE FUTURE

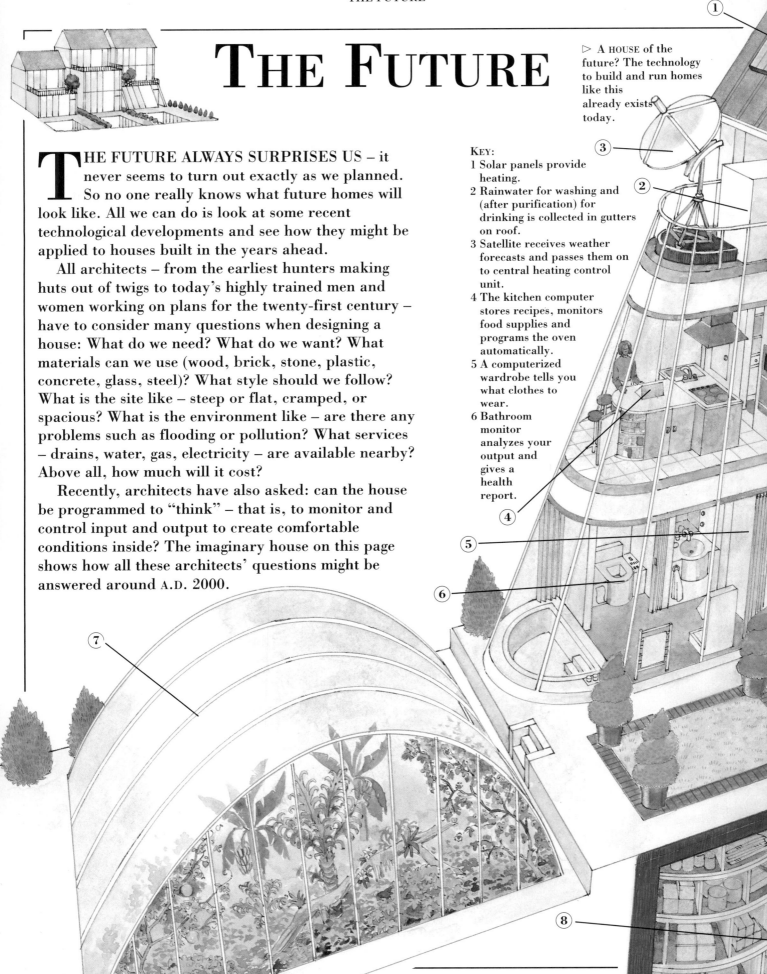

▷ A HOUSE of the future? The technology to build and run homes like this already exists today.

THE FUTURE ALWAYS SURPRISES US – it never seems to turn out exactly as we planned. So no one really knows what future homes will look like. All we can do is look at some recent technological developments and see how they might be applied to houses built in the years ahead.

All architects – from the earliest hunters making huts out of twigs to today's highly trained men and women working on plans for the twenty-first century – have to consider many questions when designing a house: What do we need? What do we want? What materials can we use (wood, brick, stone, plastic, concrete, glass, steel)? What style should we follow? What is the site like – steep or flat, cramped, or spacious? What is the environment like – are there any problems such as flooding or pollution? What services – drains, water, gas, electricity – are available nearby? Above all, how much will it cost?

Recently, architects have also asked: can the house be programmed to "think" – that is, to monitor and control input and output to create comfortable conditions inside? The imaginary house on this page shows how all these architects' questions might be answered around A.D. 2000.

KEY:
1 Solar panels provide heating.
2 Rainwater for washing and (after purification) for drinking is collected in gutters on roof.
3 Satellite receives weather forecasts and passes them on to central heating control unit.
4 The kitchen computer stores recipes, monitors food supplies and programs the oven automatically.
5 A computerized wardrobe tells you what clothes to wear.
6 Bathroom monitor analyzes your output and gives a health report.

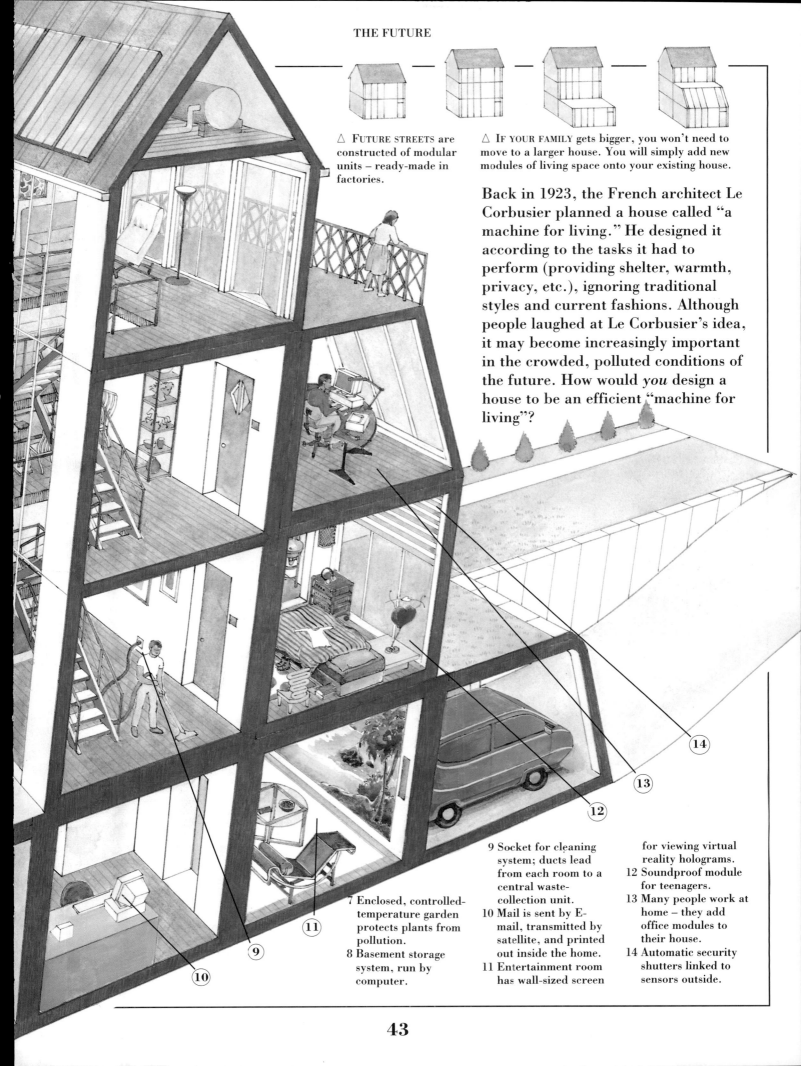

THE FUTURE

△ FUTURE STREETS are constructed of modular units – ready-made in factories.

△ IF YOUR FAMILY gets bigger, you won't need to move to a larger house. You will simply add new modules of living space onto your existing house.

Back in 1923, the French architect Le Corbusier planned a house called "a machine for living." He designed it according to the tasks it had to perform (providing shelter, warmth, privacy, etc.), ignoring traditional styles and current fashions. Although people laughed at Le Corbusier's idea, it may become increasingly important in the crowded, polluted conditions of the future. How would *you* design a house to be an efficient "machine for living"?

7 Enclosed, controlled-temperature garden protects plants from pollution.
8 Basement storage system, run by computer.
9 Socket for cleaning system; ducts lead from each room to a central waste-collection unit.
10 Mail is sent by E-mail, transmitted by satellite, and printed out inside the home.
11 Entertainment room has wall-sized screen for viewing virtual reality holograms.
12 Soundproof module for teenagers.
13 Many people work at home – they add office modules to their house.
14 Automatic security shutters linked to sensors outside.

Timeline

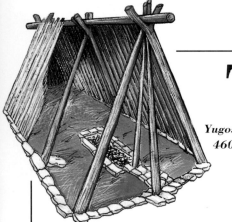

Yugoslavian shelter, 4600 B.C.

B.C.

c.300,000 The first known houses – shelters made of twigs and brushwood – are made by tribes of hunters. The earliest example so far discovered comes from Terra Amata in southern France.

c.35,000-10,000 Ice Age hunters who live in areas where there are no trees make semi-permanent tents, designed to stay in place for a whole winter season, using enormous mammoth skins and bones.

Dutch village house, 4000 B.C.

c.30,000 Wandering hunters cross the frozen Bering Sea to reach America from Siberia. They become the first Americans. They build simple shelters from anything they can find – wood, earth, twigs, skins.

c.12,000 Nomadic hunting communities in Europe build winter camps for extended family groups, using timber cut from dense forests nearby.

c.6000 The earliest-known towns develop, on the fertile banks of great rivers in the Middle East, especially in present-day Iraq. In Turkey, the trading town of Catal Hüyük contains closely-packed houses, with separate rooms marked out for working, sleeping, and worshipping. They are entered through a hole in the roof.

c.5500 In Mediterranean regions, where the warm climate makes it a healthy and pleasant place to live, large village communities begin to develop. They live in houses made of mud bricks, close to their fields and flocks.

c.5000 Fisher families on the shores of the Danube River (present-day Hungary and former Yugoslavia) build solid huts out of wooden logs covered with turf. They also build smokehouses nearby, to preserve the fish they have caught.

c.4000 In China, hunting and fishing communities build pyramid-shaped huts out of clay and straw. Already, there is a difference in size and strength between houses belonging to poor people and those of village leaders.

c.4000 In colder northern Europe, village people build houses of timber, with thatched roofs. These are the only usable building materials they can find in the forests.

c.3000 Elsewhere in central Europe, houses are built on stilts above lakes, for safety.

Greek pottery models, 100 B.C.

c.3000 The Inuit people reach Alaska and the Canadian Arctic from Siberia. They bring traditional designs for houses – snow igloos and underground earth shelters.

c.2500 Inhabitants of the cities of Mohenjo-daro, Kalibangan, and Harappa, in the Indus Valley (north India), live in large courtyard houses built beside planned city streets, with efficient drainage and public baths.

c.1800 Fishing communities in the bleak, windswept Orkney Islands build entire houses and all their furniture out of rough-hewn stone.

c.1700 The palace of King Minos is built on the Greek island of Crete. Rich Cretans appreciate colorful, elegant interior decoration and comforts such as baths and running water.

c.1500 Mini-palaces are built by wealthy citizens in Egypt. Ordinary people live in smaller, more crowded homes.

c.1500 Olmec peoples build palaces of carefully shaped stone in Central America.

c.1400 Pharaoh Akenhaten of Egypt begins new capital city at Amarna with planned housing; it is later abandoned.

c.1000 On the Greek mainland, warrior kings build citadels of massive stone, as at Mycenae. In the countryside, farmers live in simple, stone-built houses.

c.1000 First huts of wood and straw built on the site of the future city of Rome.

c.900 Pima Native American peoples build houses of twigs interlaced with reeds, covered with earth.

c.600 First public water supply arranged for inhabitants of Athens, Greece.

c.500 Celts build wood-and-thatch round houses and stone hill-forts in northern Europe.

c.400 Inhabitants of Greek city-states live in well-planned courtyard homes.

c.200 First known paved streets built between houses in Rome.

Roman furniture, A.D. 100

Chinese courtyard house, A.D. 100

c.1 Comfortable homes built for rich citizens of Roman provincial towns like Pompeii and Herculaneum (both destroyed by volcanic eruption in A.D. 79). Ordinary citizens live in smaller houses, or, more often, rented single rooms.

Native American tipis

A.D.

c.1 By now, many traditional styles of African and North American house building are probably well established.

c.100 Chinese farmers build courtyard homes with integral watchtowers, lavatories, and pigsties.

c.100 Roman "insulae" (apartment buildings) built in crowded ports and cities.

c.100 Roman villas (country houses) built in the lands surrounding Rome, and in conquered territories ruled as part of the Roman Empire.

c.500 Germanic villagers (Saxons, Angles, Franks, Jutes) build homes of timber posts, with wattle-and-daub walls and grass-thatched roofs. Some are partly sunken underground.

Norman manor house, 1200

c.500 After centuries of unrest and migration, Mongol peoples develop a regular nomadic lifestyle, traveling the great plains of Central Asia, living in portable gers.

c.700 In Muslim lands throughout the Middle East and Africa, houses are built in traditional styles, using designs pioneered by the Egyptians and the civilizations of early Iraq. Many have devices such as wind chimneys, to keep them cool.

c.700 Troglodytes make their homes in caves in Turkey and Central Asia. Cave dwellings and temples are also constructed in China.

Native American house, 1600

c.800 The Maya of Central America build magnificent stone palaces for their kings and simple mud-brick houses for ordinary people.

c.800 Vikings build solid timber and stone houses, designed to withstand the winter cold. Many have built-in furniture, for example, beds lining the living room walls. In areas settled by the Vikings, where no trees grow, houses are built of stone plus slabs of turf.

c.900 Muslim houses in southern Spain and northern and eastern Africa are built to mirror traditional values, such as privacy for women, family solidarity, and generous hospitality.

German merchant's house, 15th century

c.1000 Pueblo villages are built in the American Southwest.

c.1100 Norman lords, conquerors of England, begin to build simple castles as strongholds and as their homes.

c.1200 In European cities, wealthy lords, merchants, and bankers build fine stone houses in towns. Ordinary people live in simple houses, made of timber framing, wattle-and-daub.

c.1400 Prosperous houses in European villages and towns now strong and well built, of timber or stone. They

Renaissance bed

are often workshops or places of business as well as somewhere to live.

c.1450 Earthquake-proof homes built by Incas in Peru. The Aztecs of Mexico build homes of thatch and mud brick.

c.1450 Teahouses begin to be added to wealthy houses in Japan.

c.1500 Fired clay brick begins to be widely used for building houses in northern Europe.

c.1550 The first European "stately homes" are built.

c.1600 Early European settlers in America build simple log cabins or sod houses.

c.1750 Rich districts of many European and American towns are rebuilt in elegant style. In the countryside, landowners build fine new country houses, or remodel their ancestral homes.

Indian village house, 1760

c.1800 The Industrial Revolution encourages millions of workers to move to the cities, in search of work in factories. They are housed in unhealthy, crowded slums or tenement buildings.

In the country, rural workers continue to live in traditional-style homes; conditions for most are miserable.

c.1870 The first modern suburbs are built on the outskirts of cities. Comfortable country villas for middle-class families are also designed at this time. Soon, whole "garden cities" are planned, giving all inhabitants fresh air and a pleasant environment.

18th-century American farm

c.1890 Fashionable parts of European cities are rebuilt with apartment houses, in the latest artistic styles.

c.1900 American architects build skyscrapers, using new construction techniques based on steel, glass, and concrete. These ideas are copied worldwide.

c.1920s European architects, led by Le Corbusier, begin to build tall high-rise buildings.

1930s German and Scandinavian architects build homes to simple, dramatic, open-plan designs.

Apartment building in Paris, 1902

c.1950s Large-scale projects to rebuild homes in Russia and Europe, following World War II.

c.1960s In Britain, Canada, the United States, and Australia developers build collections of identical new houses ("developments") designed for families.

Suburban British house, 1930s

c.1970s High-rises are criticized. Growing awareness of vast gap between housing available to rich and poor people.

c.1980s "Intelligent" houses built in Japan and Europe.

Habitat '67, Montreal, Canada

GLOSSARY

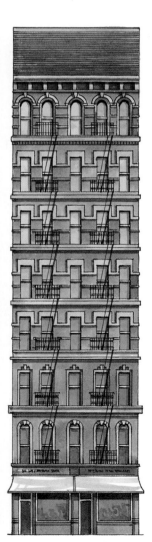

Amphitheater Circular sports arena with an open space surrounded by rows of seats.

Art nouveau A style of building and decoration based on flowing curves and lines, popular in Europe around 1900.

Arts and crafts A style of building based on traditional English designs, popular around 1900.

Atrium A central courtyard. Roman atriums were open to the sky; modern atriums usually have high glass roofs.

Barracks Large buildings where groups of people - usually soldiers or slaves – sleep and relax off duty.

Battlements A well-defended walkway around the top of castle walls.

Brushwood Twigs and small branches.

Butler A senior household servant, always a man. In charge of wine, silver, dishes, and other household valuables.

Daub Mud or clay mixed with straw and horsehair.

Drawbridge A wooden bridge guarding the entrance to a castle; it could be raised and lowered.

Ducts Pipes and channels built within floors and walls.

E-mail Letters sent electronically by computers linked together in a network.

Footings Solid base at the bottom of a wall.

Frankish Belonging to the Franks, early inhabitants of northern France and southern Germany.

Frescoes Wall paintings, made on a surface of fresh, smooth plaster.

Ger The portable home – like a big tent – used by Mongol nomads in Central Asia.

Ginna House built for a priest of the Dogon people of West Africa.

Grooms Servants who take care of horses.

Hallboy Junior servant who ran errands, fetched and carried, and cleaned shoes.

Hall house A medieval single-story house containing one big room (a hall) open to the roof, plus smaller rooms.

Hogan A house of earth and brushwood made by Native Americans.

Ice Age The period in prehistory when large areas of the earth's surface were covered by ice.

Industrial Revolution The period approximately 1750-1850, when many new machines were invented.

Insulation A barrier (for example, a thick wall) designed to enclose a space and protect it from changes in temperature.

Keep The central building of a castle.

Khana The collapsible wooden framework used to support a ger.

Kiva An underground meeting room, built by Native Americans of the Pueblo tribe.

Limewash A mixture of crushed, burnt limestone and water.

Loess Fine, dusty soil, found in layers several feet thick in parts of China. It can be excavated to make underground homes.

Longhouse A house that contains several units, either for housing several families, or for a family and their animals.

Loom A machine used for weaving cloth. Until the Industrial Revolution, looms were powered by hand.

Manor house Large house built for a lord who owned a manor – a medieval great estate.

Medieval The period approximately A.D. 1000-1500.

Paleolithic Belonging to the Old Stone Age (before 5000 B.C.).

Parlor ("room for talking") A private sitting room.

Pelts Skins and furs of animals.

Portcullis A strong metal grille barrier that guarded the entrance to a castle.

Pueblo The name of Native American nations who live in villages made of many small houses linked together, plus larger communal buildings. The word is also used to describe the houses themselves.

Raja An Indian word for "king."

Scullery maid A servant who did all the rough work (washing up, etc.) in a kitchen.

Sod house A house built from slabs of earth, with grass still growing in them. Built in parts of America where there was no stone or timber.

Solar A private sitting room, often used only by women.

Steppes Wide, open grasslands.

Stockade A strong fence.

Suburb Area of housing on the outskirts of a town.

Tallow Sheep's fat.

Tenement An apartment house for workers; often poorly built, dangerous, and unhealthy to live in.

Terrace Row of houses joined together side by side.

Threshold The area at the bottom of a doorway.

Timber-framed A method of construction using strong wooden uprights and a "filling" of wattle-and-daub for walls.

Tipi A portable tent, used by some Native American nations.

Troglodyte Someone who lives in a cave.

Tweenie Maid who did heavy housework plus lighter duties, such as waiting at table.

Wattle A network of sticks, covered in daub (mud) to make a wall.

INDEX

Page numbers in bold refer to illustrations.